Criss
Angel

Gail B. Stewart

Mason Crest Publishers

Produced by OTTN Publishing in association with
21st Century Publishing and Communications, Inc.

MASON CREST PUBLISHERS INC.
370 Reed Road
Broomall, Pennsylvania 19008
(866) MCP-BOOK (toll free)
www.masoncrest.com

Printed in the United States of America.

First Printing

9 8 7 6 5 4 3 2 1

Library of Congress Cataloging-in-Publication Data

Stewart, Gail B. (Gail Barbara), 1949–
    Criss Angel / Gail B. Stewart.
       p. cm. — (Modern role models)
    Includes bibliographical references.
ISBN-13: 978-1-4222-0497-9 (hardcover) — ISBN-13: 978-1-4222-0784-0 (pbk.)
ISBN-10: 1-4222-0497-9 (hardcover)
 1. Angel, Criss—Juvenile literature. 2. Magicians—United States—Biography—
Juvenile literature. I. Title.
GV1545.A64S74 2009
793.8092—dc22
[B]   2008020415

Publisher's note:
All quotations in this book come from original sources, and contain the spelling
and grammatical inconsistencies of the original text.

CROSS-CURRENTS

In the ebb and flow of the currents of life we are each influenced
by many people, places, and events that we directly experience
or have learned about. Throughout the chapters of this book you
will come across CROSS-CURRENTS reference boxes. These
boxes direct you to a CROSS-CURRENTS section in the back
of the book that contains fascinating and informative sidebars
and related pictures. Go on. ▸▸

CONTENTS

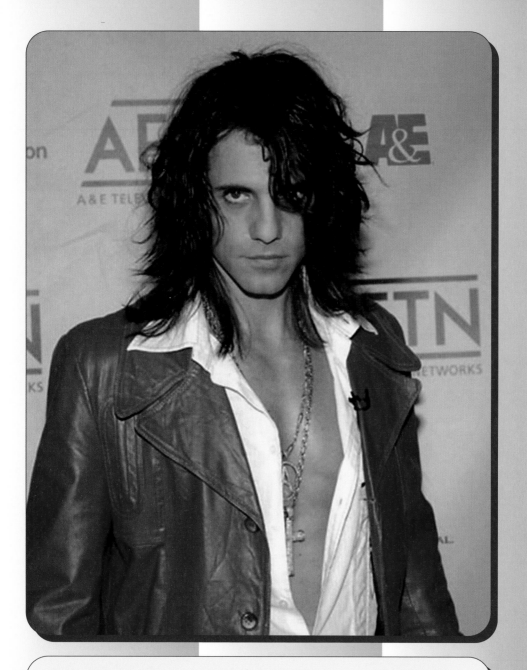

Criss Angel appears at the A&E Television network's Upfront Celebration, held April 21, 2005, at Rockefeller Center, in New York City. That July, his new series, *Criss Angel: Mindfreak*, would debut on A&E. In two weeks the show drew 1.7 million viewers—many more people than the average for the cable network's regular audience.

1

How Did He Do That?

CRISS ANGEL WAS RIDING HIGH IN THE SUMMER of 2005. He was on the verge of making the leap from being a fairly well-known entertainer to a white-hot star. It was in 2005 that the 37-year-old magician who had been amazing audiences for years had been signed by the A&E cable network to do his own television series.

The series, called *Criss Angel: Mindfreak*, would reach millions of people each week. Each half-hour episode would feature his unique style of magic—part **illusion**; part street magic; part seemingly impossible, death-defying stunts. And behind it all, Criss would supply a pounding backdrop of rock music.

In July, shortly before the season premiere of *Mindfreak*, Angel appeared at a press conference to talk about the new show. Without warning, he downed a shot of wine that contained several sharp sewing needles. As reporters looked on in horror, Angel calmly swallowed some thread. In a few moments, he lifted his shirt and began to slowly pull the thread, now with the needles dangling from it, from his belly button.

⇒ A NEW KIND OF MAGIC ⇐

This trick was meant to give the press an idea of what his magic is all about. If reporters thought *Mindfreak* was going to be a typical magic show, they needed to think again. As Angel told *Forbes* magazine reporter Susan Karlin, people no longer want to watch "typical" magic:

> **❝Magic is a wonderful art form, but it needs to be updated. I grew up on MTV and wanted to break the caricature of a magician pulling rabbits out of a hat or shoving a girl in leotards in a box. Why are magicians still doing what they did 100 years ago?❞**

But no matter what tricks and stunts he performed, a viewer could merely look at Criss Angel to see that this was no traditional magician. In fact, with his shaggy dark hair, sparkly jewelry, and his six-pack abs (he frequently removes his shirt for his stunts), Angel looks more like a rock-star idol than a magician. No ordinary magician? No kidding!

⇒ WOWING THE AUDIENCES ⇐

It did not take long for A&E to realize that its decision to feature Criss Angel weekly was a smart one. In fact, the premiere of *Mindfreak* brought in 1.7 million viewers. A&E's average viewing audience for a prime-time show is 1.1 million. What made the cable network executives even more excited was the huge number of younger viewers. The average age of the network's viewers is nearly 50. But Angel's show lowered that average to 34. That meant that A&E was drawing in a wider age range of people—a good thing for any television network.

Some of the buzz about Criss Angel had to do with his fearlessness. Every week he put himself in harm's way, doing something that audiences had never seen before. In the season premiere, he set himself ablaze, without face protection. It was his mother's

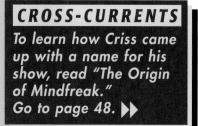

CROSS-CURRENTS

To learn how Criss came up with a name for his show, read "The Origin of Mindfreak."
Go to page 48. ▶▶

70th birthday, he explained to the crowd that had gathered, and he wanted to turn himself into a human birthday candle for her. In another episode, he looked for a way to update the idea of lying on a bed of sharp nails. Angel decided that the trick would be more amazing if he could also support the weight of an 8,500-pound Humvee as he lay on the razor sharp, 8-inch nails. Onlookers watched, screaming and wincing, as Angel's body—stripped to the waist—absorbed the weight of the huge vehicle.

A cameraman films a scene from *Criss Angel: Mindfreak.* Criss is an illusionist. He does not claim to have any super-natural powers. But he survives death-defying stunts, like being impaled on a spiked fence, setting himself on fire, being buried alive, and being run over by a Hummer while lying on a bed of nails.

In a *Mindfreak* episode broadcast during the show's second season, in 2006, Criss amazes swimmers by walking on water at the swimming pool at the Aladdin Resort and Casino in Las Vegas, Nevada. Stunts for many of the show's first two seasons were filmed at the Aladdin; subsequent episodes have been set at the Luxor Las Vegas.

⇒ "This Is So Weird! This Is So Bizarre!" ⇐

But the death-defying spectacles were not the only things audiences loved about the new show. In each episode Angel would take his act to the streets and parks of Las Vegas. He loved the challenge of doing his magic away from the stage, just connecting with people at random.

In one episode from *Mindfreak*'s first season, Angel introduced himself to a group of tourists in a Las Vegas park. He asked three of them if they would support his head and hold his hands as he bent backward, his feet on the ground. After a few moments, he told them to step away. The crowd, aghast, watched as instead of falling backward, Angel's position never changed. More unbelievably, he raised one leg, leaving the other on the ground. He seemed to be **levitating**—floating on air! The stunned onlookers checked underneath Angel's body for wires, supports, or other tricks. But there was nothing there.

Carolyn Spencer of Chicago was in Las Vegas during the filming of the episode. She watched firsthand as Angel appeared to levitate as he was going up an escalator. Later, she described the reaction of the people nearby:

> **"If you're watching it on TV, you probably say, it's fake. It's a camera stunt. Or it's some kind of computerized trick. But really, I was there. My friend and I saw him do it. He was floating a few inches off the step of the escalator.**
>
> **People around us were amazed, saying, 'This is so weird, this is so bizarre!' I've never, never seen anything like this before. I mean, people were literally gaping. "**

This new show seemed to defy the laws of gravity. Levitation is not real. Or is it? For viewers, the line had been blurred between possible and impossible. But as each week's show continued to draw a bigger and bigger audience, at least one thing was very clear. Criss Angel had definitely arrived. And people could not get enough of him.

Born Christopher Sarantakos, Criss Angel is the youngest of three sons in a close Greek-American family. He grew up in East Meadow, New York, on Long Island. According to one story, he took his stage name when a fellow magician told him he looked nothing like an angel. In 2005 he told *USA Today* that Criss Angel is now his real name.

Early Tricks

CRISS ANGEL BECAME INTERESTED IN MAGIC when he was very young. Of course, he did not call himself Criss Angel then. That is a stage name. Christopher Nicholas Sarantakos was born on December 19, 1967, in Long Island, New York. He was the youngest of three sons born to Greek American parents John and Dimitra Sarantakos.

As Criss grew up, he wanted to try every activity or sport his older brothers, J. D. and Costa, did. Both J. D. and Costa took music lessons, so Criss wanted to do the same. His parents bought him a little drum set and were pleased to see that he had a knack for the instrument. In fact, obtaining that drum set sparked a lively interest in rock music that would play a big part in Criss's life.

⟫ "I BEGGED AND BEGGED" ⟪

When Criss was seven years old, his Aunt Stella showed him a card trick. In his autobiography, *Mindfreak: Secret Revelations*,

Angel recalls that he knew right away that it was something he wanted to learn:

> **"It just boggled my mind. I had to know how she did it. I bugged Aunt Stella for hours. . . . I begged and begged until she couldn't take another minute of my asking and finally gave in. From that day on, I was hooked. Once she shared the secret of the trick, I felt this incredible sense of power that an adult didn't understand how it worked, but *I* did."**

From that day on, Criss began focusing on magic. He wanted to learn more tricks, to perform before audiences, and to become the best magician in the world. While his friends were playing or hanging out, Criss spent his free time at home, learning more tricks and reading about famous magicians. He spent his entire five-dollar-per-week allowance buying tricks from a nearby magic store.

CROSS-CURRENTS

To learn about a magician who had a great influence on Criss Angel's career, read "The Greatest Ever." Go to page 48. ▶▶

⇒ A WORKING MAGICIAN ⇐

Criss had his first paying job as a magician when he was twelve. The event was a birthday party in his neighborhood. Looking back, he says the tricks and his performance were not very good, but at the time he was thrilled. He was paid $10, and he could hardly wait to get another chance.

When he was 14, Criss began working at a nearby restaurant. He would walk from table to table and perform magic tricks for the guests. He made about $100 each week and recycled most of his earnings into more equipment for the illusions he was designing. It was fun just imagining people watching him do the next impossible trick.

What was *not* possible, Criss knew, was to continue his education after high school. He had merely tolerated his time at East Meadow High School. While he had been physically in class, mentally he was busy thinking about his next performance or a new trick he could try. After he graduated, he intended to begin his career full-time.

CROSS-CURRENTS

If you'd like to learn more about Criss's early determination to become famous, check out "Fantasizing." Go to page 50. ▶▶

Criss poses with his mother, Dimitra Sarantakos, at the April 1, 2006, event where he received the 2005 Magician of the Year title from Hollywood's famous Magic Castle (Academy of Magical Arts and Sciences). After high school Criss wanted to work full-time as a magician. By age 19 he was making $3,000 a week performing at children's parties and nightclubs.

Though his parents were somewhat disappointed that going to college was of no interest to their son, they supported his ambition.

⇒ "I Was Relentless" ⇐

Angel continued his magic, but in the 1990s he started combining it with the hard-rock music he loved. Using animals, **pyrotechnics**, and strange-looking masks, he performed magic while singing and playing in his band. He had a Goth-type look, with dark eye makeup, leather clothing, and waist-length hair. In an interview with Cleveland's *Plain Dealer*, he explains that young audiences really seemed to enjoy seeing something more interesting than simply rock music:

CRISS ANGEL

In the 1990s Criss transformed his hard-rock music and his magic stunts into a theatrical experience. He explained to *Forbes* magazine in 2005: "I wanted to combine magic and music in a much grander vision that required a band, larger illusions and more equipment." As a rock-star version of a magician, he wore his hair long and dressed in black.

> **Kids get fed enough by just watching MTV and listening to their CDs. . . . [They don't] want to come out and spend money that they don't have to see a show that really is not a theatrical experience.**

Angel continued to publicize himself, making flyers, putting ads in the newspaper—anything that would help him get in front of an audience. He had no money to hire a public relations staff or even a manager. Every penny he earned went back into his show—buying tricks, equipment, and more publicity.

By the mid-1990s, however, the work began to pay off. In 1994 Criss was given a spot doing magic on an ABC television special called *Secrets*. He even found a way to get his story told on a popular syndicated show called *A Current Affair*.

In 1998 Criss got a bigger break. Madison Square Garden, the huge arena in New York City, turned itself into a huge haunted fun house during the Halloween season. Angel talked the producers into letting him perform 10-minute shows throughout the day, totaling 60 performances daily. Over 12 days, more than 80,000 people flocked to see his shows. To make more money, he printed up Criss Angel baseball caps and T-shirts to sell and took in more than $50,000.

However, the year 1998 was also a time of great loss. Angel's father, who had been battling stomach cancer, died. It was a blow to the entire family, which had counted on John Sarantakos for strength and good humor. Angel, especially, had always relied on his father for advice and support in his career. Instead of withdrawing into his grief, however, Criss threw himself into his work. In his autobiography, he writes:

> **Everything I do, I do for him. I dedicate my life, my art, my success, and my love to my father. It is my greatest disappointment that my dad isn't here to see what I'm doing.**

Little did Criss realize at the time, but many of his most famous stunts would be inspired by his father's struggle with cancer.

Criss Angel stands in front of the World Underground Theater at the World Wrestling Federation complex in Times Square, New York. In December 2001, the illusionist created, directed, and produced a one-act off-Broadway show that he performed at the 150-seat theater. He would give nearly 600 performances of the show, which he called *Mindfreak*, before it closed in January 2003.

Mindfreak

THE MONEY CRISS ANGEL EARNED AT THE MADISON Square Garden Halloween event was helpful. It gave him cash to invest in more illusions. But it also reminded him that his real goal was to create his own show, not merely appear in other shows. Since he was a little boy, he had been dreaming of the day he could walk out on the stage he designed and do tricks and illusions that were created for that space. So far, however, he had not had that chance.

⇒ THE WRONG TIME? ⇐

Shortly after the terrorist attacks on September 11, 2001, Angel made a decision. He wanted to put on his own **off-Broadway** show, and he believed this was the time. But it would be an expensive **venture**. Just renting a theater in New York would cost more money than he had.

CROSS-CURRENTS

Criss Angel was not an immediate success. For insight into his feelings about his struggle for fame, read "Rejection." Go to page 51. ▶▶

Criss tried to find investors who would help, but he had little success. Everyone he talked to was nervous. People were worried that there would be more attacks. They were not eager to see a Broadway show. Tourists, who usually made up a large part of the audiences, were not visiting the city. Normally an exciting, thriving place, much of Broadway had gone "dark" since the attacks. It seemed the wrong time to open a new show.

But Angel believed his show would draw people. He went to his mother and asked if he could mortgage the family home for cash. His mother had always had confidence in her son's future as a performer, and she agreed with the plan. With about $300,000 borrowed against his mother's house, Angel excitedly began creating his show.

⟫ OPENING ⟪

Criss Angel's *Mindfreak* opened on December 13, 2001, at the Underground Theater in Times Square. The set was dark and creepy, and Angel shared the stage with a number of invented characters—some that looked like animals from other worlds, others like scary spacemen.

Angel had spent money hiring the best production people around. The surreal-looking creatures had been designed and constructed by Steve Johnson, who had done such work in the hit movie *Men in Black*. For the **choreography** of the creatures, Angel had retained the services of Debra Brown, who had worked with Cirque du Soleil. The effects were stunning, and the audience was enthralled.

Angel's illusions included a number of card tricks, a levitation, and various disappearances. He also did a spectacular Houdini-type escape from a straitjacket while hanging upside down. One of the most popular bits, however, was more funny than scary. He invited a volunteer from the audience to come onstage. As Criss did a trick that totally baffled the volunteer, he allowed everyone in the audience to see exactly how he carried out the illusion.

Mindfreak became amazingly popular. Ticket sales rose as word spread about this talented and engaging young magician. Angel's success was recognized by his fellow magicians, too. In 2001 he was awarded Magician of the Year by the International Magicians Society.

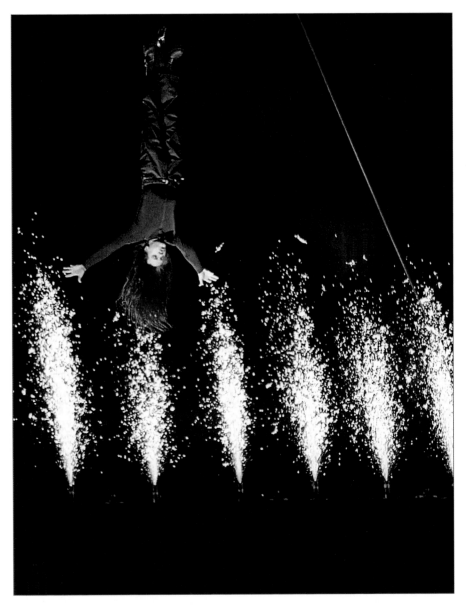

A routine stunt popularized by early 20th-century escape artist Harry Houdini, breaking out of a straitjacket is also a Criss Angel standard. But he has been known to add even more danger. In this January 2003 photo, taken in sub-freezing temperatures in Milwaukee, Wisconsin, Angel has just broken free while dangling by his feet 100 feet above a crowd.

⚛ FACING FEARS ⚛

Criss had hoped *Mindfreak* could run three months, but it lasted longer. In the the spring of 2002, *Mindfreak* was still generating lots of excitement. During the summer, Angel began to explore ways to promote the show even more. He had already increased the physical challenges in his performances, but he wanted to try something new. Instead of performing an illusion of risk, he wanted to create a demonstration that was a painful test of real danger.

Criss had been inspired by a documentary he had seen about coming-of-age rituals in various cultures around the world. One of these rituals was extreme body piercing, which intrigued him. He thought about what it would be like to hang by hooks that had been pierced in his skin. In years past, such an idea would have made him queasy. However, as he explained in an interview with Underground Online, watching his father fight the pain of cancer for years had had a huge impact on him:

> **"He believed that his body was a slave to his mind. He didn't care what the doctors said [when they told him he had only three weeks to live] and was able to live more than three years. . . . When my father died . . . , I realized that I needed to face my own fears. People don't know this, but I used to pass out when I used to get blood taken at the doctor's. "**

Angel believed that he could confront his fear of needles while at the same time offering his audiences a new type of spectacle. He contacted an expert on body piercing and **suspension** and set about learning how it was done.

⚛ HANGING AROUND TIMES SQUARE ⚛

On February 20, 2002, Angel's team prepared him for the stunt, which would take place at the corner of 43rd and Broadway. He would hang in what was called the "Superman position"—two large fishhooks in the skin of his shoulders, two in the middle of his back, two in his lower back, and the last two **embedded** in his calves. His goal would be to hang for six hours, which would break the current record for someone being suspended in that way.

The hooks had to be placed just right, as he had learned. If they were too deep, they could do permanent damage to the muscles of his body. If they were not deep enough, the weight of his body would cause them to rip from his skin. After the hooks were in, his team attached them to the harnesses and he began his suspension—eight feet above the ground.

Over the next six hours, more than 75,000 people came to watch. As Angel explains in his autobiography, he knew some people would be skeptical, thinking that the stunt was merely an illusion:

Criss hangs suspended from eight giant fishhooks attached to his legs and back during a test of endurance that took place on February 20, 2002, in the window of the World Wrestling Federation (WWF) Times Square store in New York City. Angel performed the Body Suspension stunt for passersby to promote his off-Broadway show *Mindfreak*.

"Some people claimed I wore a skin suit or some kind of false skin. I'd like to know what a skin suit is, because I'd happily sign up for one. It would have been . . . a lot easier! Some people even suggested I was a **hologram**, so I began to spin . . . to make people believe I wasn't some projected image."

ANOTHER *MINDFREAK*

The body-suspension spectacle—which did break the world's record—had another positive effect. It generated lots of publicity about Criss Angel, and about his off-Broadway show. *Mindfreak* had been doing fine at the box office up until then, but after the Times Square stunt, Angel began playing to packed audiences.

Television executives were also beginning to take notice of Criss Angel. The ABC network signed him to do a one-hour show during its *13 Nights of Halloween* special to be broadcast in October 2002. One of the stunts he performed for that special was filmed in August—also in Times Square.

The stunt was called "Submerged," and it was Angel's tribute to the great Harry Houdini, who had performed the trick 75 years before. He had been bound and **shackled** in a water tank. He had to free himself from the shackles and emerge from the tank before his breath ran out.

Angel decided to update the trick. Like Houdini, he would be tightly chained and shackled in a 220-gallon tank. However, Criss would have a breathing tube and would have to remain in the water for 24 hours. When that time had elapsed, his breathing tube would be cut off, and he would have to escape quickly, in full view of the spectators in Times Square. "Submerged" would not only test his ability to escape quickly, but it also would be a grueling test of endurance.

A BOW AND A FAINT

The trick almost proved to be too much, even though Angel had worked hard to prepare for it. He developed a blinding headache because of the pressure of being underwater for so long. At one point, the water **filtration** system stopped working. The water became cloudy because of the buildup of his shedding skin cells. The

Criss prepares to submerge himself, chained and shackled, in a tank of water for 24 hours. His underwater escape act, performed on August 26, 2002, was filmed as part of his first television special, *Criss Angel: Mindfreak*, which was broadcast during ABC's *13 Nights of Halloween*. Attending the stunt were his mother, Dimitra Sarantakos, and brothers Costa and J. D.

As Criss's fame grew, the illusionist's face appeared on the cover of *Genii* magazine in its December 2003 issue. *Genii* is the longest-running independent magazine devoted to magic and magicians. Its editor, Richard Kaufman, would later tell *USA Today* in a story about Angel: "He is on track to be the next superstar in our field."

worst, however, was when the water became too warm. His team had to add buckets of ice water to the tank so he would not pass out.

Criss stayed in the tank for 24 hours, however, as the large crowds cheered him on. And when his oxygen was turned off, he was able to perform his escape. When he first burst from the tank, he was triumphant. He waved and grinned at all the fans who had supported him. He spoke with reporters. And then, suddenly, he passed out. His brother J. D., one of his team members, recalls that frightening moment in Angel's autobiography:

> **When Christopher made his escape, he was high from the adrenaline. He did a television interview and then walked twenty feet outside to thank the fans and media. He came back inside, took two steps, and collapsed in my arms. It was terrifying and emotionally draining.**

Luckily, the team had had arranged for an ambulance to be on hand, just in case something went wrong. Paramedics took him to a nearby hospital, where he was treated for exhaustion and hypothermia—a condition in which the body cannot stay warm enough.

Angel's mother, who had been at Times Square watching her son, told a reporter from the *New York Daily News* how frightened she had been:

> **He was white, and he wouldn't respond at all. I just wanted to see him breathe.**

⇒ OUT OF DEBT ⇐

Criss Angel recovered quickly from his medical problems. "Submerged" had been successful. He had received a great deal of national publicity during his time in the water tank. Shows such as *Good Morning America* covered it live, and newspapers featured him on the front page. And "Submerged" helped give his ABC Halloween special for *13 Nights of Halloween* the highest rating of all the shows in that series.

When the off-Broadway show finally closed a few months later, in January 2003, it had taken in millions of dollars. Criss had hoped it could run 3 months, but it ran for more than 14 months, with 600 performances. Its success meant he could repay the loan on his mother's house. He also had money to invest in plans for more illusions and more events. Angel was delighted, and he could hardly wait to see what the future would bring.

CROSS-CURRENTS

Criss has given hints about future stunts in interviews. To learn about some of his ideas, read "A Learning Process." Go to page 52. ▶▶

A promotional poster for the Sci Fi Channel 2003 Halloween Special entitled *Criss Angel: Supernatural.* Criss was in great demand when he appeared on the show, which was broadcast on Halloween night. He had landed gigs with several other cable television networks, including TBS in Japan, MTV, and Discovery Channel.

4

A New Start

AFTER THE ABC HALLOWEEN SPECIAL, CRISS received more offers from television executives. In 2003 the Sci Fi Channel asked him to do another Halloween special. Criss and his team worked hard to create an astonishing show. The special, called *Supernatural*, featured an amazing trick in which Angel appeared to walk up the side of a building.

⇒ UNHAPPY ⇐

The executives at the Sci Fi Channel had promised to do a lot of advance publicity for the show. That was important to Angel, who saw any performance as a steppingstone to further his career. But as the airing date approached, Angel was disappointed. There was little publicity for *Supernatural*. In his autobiography, Criss wrote that he felt misled:

❝I enlisted the help of my brothers and cousins, and together as a family we worked around the clock to give the Sci Fi Channel the best Halloween special we could. Even though they promised to **allocate** a substantial marketing budget toward the show, they ended up supporting it not at all.❞

Even without the help of publicity, however, the show was an enormous hit. It received rave reviews from media critics. But Angel was still unhappy with the channel and network executives in general. For years he had dealt with people who made promises that never came true. Some promised financial investment for his act; others guaranteed they would get back to him about a television show. Too often, such deals never happened.

⇒ "We Are Blood Brothers" ⇐

As the months went on, Angel decided he needed help. His career was moving forward, even with the broken promises he endured, but his strength was creating and designing shows that would dazzle audiences. Always a light sleeper, he was working 18 to 20 hours a day on building his act. He did not have the time or patience to work on the business end. He needed someone who could work with the owners, the investors, and the executives. That way, Angel could focus on what he did best.

In 2004 Criss met Dave Baram, president of a talent management company. Called the Firm, the company managed some of the best-known stars in Hollywood—including Cameron Diaz, Robert De Niro, and Leonardo DiCaprio. Baram himself was an amateur magician who loved Angel's work. He also believed that he could help Angel get to a higher level of success.

Dave Baram was exactly the person Angel had been looking for. They created a contract, and in his autobiography Angel explained why neither of them needed to sign it:

❝From the moment I met Dave Baram . . . I knew I would be represented and managed by him for the rest of my career. We are blood brothers. We literally cut our hands, let the blood seep through, and shook on our deal. We have no paper contract. We have no need for one.❞

In addition to being an illusionist, escapologist, and stunt performer, Criss Angel is also a musician and composer. In 1998, he released *Musical Conjurings from the World of Illusion* (1998), along with his band Angeldust. Later albums have included *System 1 in the Trilogy* (2000) and the soundtracks for the off-Broadway show *Mindfreak* (2002) and for *Supernatural* (2003).

⟫ LOSING THE GOTH LOOK ⟪

Right away, Baram and Angel discussed what their goals should be. Angel was tired of doing network specials. Though he knew it might not happen right away, he wanted a long-term commitment from a network to do a series. With a weekly series, Angel would not have to introduce his style of magic to new audiences each time. The idea seemed smart to Baram, too, but he felt Angel needed to make some changes.

In the summer of 2004, Criss signed with Dave Baram's talent management agency, known as the Firm. After becoming the agency's first magician client, he made some changes to his image. He cut his waist-length hair and traded his black leather wardrobe for faded or patched jeans, t-shirts with designs, and athletic shoes.

Baram believed that Angel's image had limited his audience. The waist-length hair, the black fingernail polish, and the Goth eye makeup appealed to young viewers. Many adults, however, were not taking Angel seriously. As a result, he was not getting as large an audience as he might. Angel decided to soften his image, scaling back on the makeup. He also got rid of the nail polish and got a shorter hairstyle.

The combination of a new manager and a more appealing look worked. It was not long before the executives at A&E Television network offered Angel a series. And as the ratings for the show rose each week, he became more and more excited about this new opportunity—and the new start on his career.

❯ A LITTLE LESS DANGER ❮

After a successful first season, Angel immediately began working on taping season two. He decided there would be a change. The first season had been heavy on the danger. In addition to the Humvee and bed of nails stunt, he had performed numerous other risky spectacles.

One of the most talked-about stunts was the fishhook suspension. It was the same idea as the one he had done in Times Square in 2002. But this one was far more dangerous. Instead of spreading eight hooks evenly over his body, he would use only four hooks—all on his shoulders. Instead of hanging in the Superman position, he would be vertical. Finally, instead of hanging 8 feet off the ground, he would be lifted 1,000 feet into the air by helicopter—over the Valley of Fire in the Nevada desert.

Although Angel had survived his various stunts in season one, he decided not to perform so many in season two. He had been emphasizing the danger to get a base of fans for the series. But it was no longer necessary, he felt, to almost kill himself every week, as he told the Underground Online Web site:

> **CROSS-CURRENTS**
>
> *Criss has said that he hopes his dangerous stunts help other people. To find out how, read "Empowering the Audience." Go to page 53.* ▶▶

❝In season one it was about whether I was going to live or die each week. With season two, I really made a conscious effort to say something different and try to grow and not become a caricature of myself. I tried to do things that were much more diverse.❞

⇒ THE DISAPPEARING ELEPHANT ⇐

One illusion that was very popular with audiences in the show's second season was the disappearing elephant. Angel brought a 9,000-pound Asian elephant named Thai into the parking garage of the Aladdin Hotel in Las Vegas. He told the gathered crowd that he intended to make her disappear into thin air, but he needed their help.

Thirty or so spectators volunteered to make a human chain around Thai. They linked hands in a large circle around the elephant, and Angel told them that under no circumstances should they break their chain. Then several other people picked up long poles attached to large white sheets. This would be a screen around Thai. Angel had the screen carriers walk quickly around the elephant and then drop the screen. When the screen lay on the ground, there was no elephant. Thai had vanished!

The spectators were dumbstruck. Thai was huge and slow moving. There was no way she could have been taken out of the garage in that short time. And what about the human chain? No one had unlinked hands to let an elephant by. Some in the audience suggested that there was a trap door in the floor, but they were allowed to inspect it. There was no trap door.

One man in the audience said he was completely blown away by the demonstration. He told the cameras taping season two of *Mindfreak*:

> **❝I couldn't figure out how he did it, and neither could anyone around me. It was fantastic!❞**

⇒ MAGIC ONE ON ONE ⇐

Tricks like the vanishing elephant generated a lot of buzz in season two. But Angel continued to emphasize his street magic, too. People loved watching him close-up in malls, on the streets, and in restaurants. And they were never quite sure what would happen when he waved his hands over a woman's purse or, in one case, an almond.

In one stunt, Criss approached a couple sitting on a bench. They were sharing a bag of almonds. Angel asked if he could have one, and then he had the woman place an almond on the bench. He demonstrated that he had nothing up his sleeves and nothing in his hand. Then he waved his hand slowly over the almond—once, twice.

During the second season of *Mindfreak*, Criss made a 9,000-pound elephant named Thai disappear. The following season he had to make Thai reappear, as he explained in an interview: "I got letters from kids saying Thai was an endangered elephant on the endangered species list so I need to make the elephant come back."

Instead of an almond, a large black bug scuttled across the bench. Onlookers screamed as the woman dropped the bag of almonds.

Criss did a similar trick with a man's baseball cap. After asking the man to inspect the hat to make sure there was nothing in it, Angel asked the man to hold the cap up high over his head. He also instructed the man to think about things he feared. The man did as he was told, and then Angel had him bring the cap down slowly. When he got it to eye level, he screamed and dropped the cap. Instead of being empty, the cap now contained a large, hairy **tarantula**.

⇒ DEATH TRAP ⇐

Although Angel had cut down on the death-defying stunts, he did not eliminate them entirely. In one episode of season two, called "Death

To launch the third season of *Mindfreak*, which debuted on June 5, 2007, Criss would perform yet another death-defying stunt. A day before the broadcast, he was shackled inside a four-foot by four-foot glass cube that was encased in concrete and hoisted 40 feet off the ground. He had just 24 hours to escape before the box would come crashing down.

Trap," Angel risked his life in a whole new way. He was bound and shackled in a pine coffin, which was placed in the middle of a parking lot. At the other end of the lot, a stunt driver awaited a signal. At that moment, he was to drive full speed, directly at the coffin.

To escape being killed by the oncoming car, Angel had only seconds to get out of the shackles, kick out the side of the coffin, and roll out of the way. Manager Dave Baram explained in season two's *Mindfreak* how risky the stunt was:

> **"He has to escape and the driver's got to get his timing right. Anyone is off by a fraction of a second, and he's dead."**

As huge crowds lined the area, Angel—with chains around his neck and feet and real police handcuffs around his wrists—was sealed in the coffin. At the signal, the car roared to life. As it neared the coffin, many spectators put their hands over their eyes. They just could not watch what seemed sure to happen. But then, just a fraction of a second from certain death, Angel broke out and rolled away as the car hit the coffin. After a few moments to gather himself, Angel jumped to his feet and ran into the cheering crowd.

➤ A Success ◄

His success in season two of *Mindfreak* showed that Criss was no flash in the pan. He wasn't like some magicians, who have a limited number of tricks. He had hundreds, and hundreds more in the planning stages. He would take a short break and then begin filming season three. And his fans could not wait!

CROSS-CURRENTS

Success has made Criss Angel very wealthy. To find out how he spends his money, read "Trainfreak? Carfreak?" Go to page 54. ▶▶

The star of *Criss Angel: Mindfreak* poses for a publicity shot. In 2006, Criss told CBS News: "I'm just an artist [who] uses many different paint brushes, whether it's mentalism, hypnosis, escapes, illusion, magic, music, performance art, to try to blur the line between reality and illusion and create an experience that hopefully is engaging and connects to people."

5

Blurring the Line

THE SUCCESS OF *MINDFREAK* TURNED CRISS Angel into a real star. No longer did he have to introduce himself as he walked up to a tourist to do a little street magic. As he told one reporter from the Web site Blend Television, his fame often made his job much more difficult:

> **"The first season [of *Mindfreak*] I would go out and risk my life, and it would be a struggle to get twelve to fourteen people to watch it. Now I go out and eat an apple and two hundred people are watching."**

⇒ REAL OR FAKE? ⇐

Technology, too, was making the job more challenging. It seemed that everyone in the audience had a cell phone with a camera feature. Any misstep, any mistake in one of his illusions, Criss knew, and it would be posted on the Internet within minutes.

But instead of complaining about such challenges, Angel seemed to relish them. Just as he enjoyed doing magic on the streets, close to his audiences, he loved the challenge of having cameras around. He even provided a video camera to a volunteer at his shows, allowing him or her total access to the stunt. He called it the Spectator Point of View camera, and encouraged the volunteer to shoot from any angle. All of this, he felt, kept him sharp—and set him apart from the competition.

CROSS-CURRENTS

Criss is skeptical of people who claim to have super-natural powers. To find out why, read "Debunking the Fakes." Go to page 54. ▶▶

Some viewers say that when Criss made Thai the elephant vanish and when he levitated in midair, there was trickery involved. But Angel dismisses such comments. He maintains that much of what he does is real, such as the dangerous stunts. However, much of his act is illusion. By blurring the lines between reality and illusion, he makes the audience interested, as he explains in his autobiography:

> **The debate of real versus illusion has always intrigued me. It's what keeps my job interesting and fulfilling. . . . Look, obviously I can't make an elephant disappear, but I can create the illusion that the elephant vanished right before your eyes.**

⇒ THE LUXOR LIGHT ⇐

A spectacle that really got viewers talking occurred in the first episode of season three of *Mindfreak*. Levitations have been incredibly popular with Angel's fans. He has received thousands of requests to perform more of them—and he decided to do a spectacular levitation that seemed frightening even to him.

The location was the world-famous Luxor Hotel in Las Vegas. The Luxor is actually a glass pyramid, with brilliant spotlights that shine from the pyramid's top. The Luxor Sky Beam, as it is known, is extremely strong, burning at 42.2 billion **candlepower**. That translates to a scorching 800° Fahrenheit (427° Celsius). Angel's idea was to levitate in the light at the top of the Luxor, he explained to Blend Television reporter Steve West:

> **I thought that it would be an amazing demon-stration if one could actually float five hundred feet**

above Las Vegas Boulevard in that light, and the world [could] witness it through their eyes, through their cameras, through their video, under no control of anybody. **"**

⇒ "I COULDN'T EVEN LOOK DOWN" ⇐

That is exactly what happened. Cameras followed Angel as he made his way to the top level of the pyramid, climbing the ladder that allowed him to step outside. He stepped out, 500 feet above the busy Las Vegas Boulevard.

A nighttime photograph of the world-famous Luxor Hotel and Casino, in Las Vegas. The third season of *Criss Angel: Mindfreak* debuted with a special one-hour episode that featured Criss performing a levitation act high above the hotel, in the light emitted from the apex of the pyramid-shaped structure.

In the moments before Criss began his levitation, he spoke directly to the *Mindfreak* camera, explaining that he was well aware of the risks:

> **"If I don't get fried by the light, I could still plummet to my death for the world to see."**

But Criss was successful. As thousands of breathless spectators watched, Angel began rising in the brilliant Luxor Sky Beam. He roared with exhilaration—jubilant with the sensation. But below people looked at each other in disbelief. How was he staying aloft? Some suggested it was merely a hologram of Angel, not a living person. Others wondered if some invisible platform was lifting him up. No one knew, but they agreed that it was one of the greatest mindfreaks yet.

➢ A CHALLENGE FROM DOG ≪

Not every one of Angel's illusions or demonstrations works, of course. Most of the failures never end up on television. In season three, however, he decided to include one that actually almost killed him. It started as a good-natured bet between him and Duane Chapman, known by millions as Dog the Bounty Hunter.

Angel had a reputation as being a talented escape artist. Many of his stunts had involved his getting out of ropes, chains, and handcuffs in a short amount of time. But in his work as a bounty hunter, Chapman had had to subdue thousands of fugitives. He had developed skills in tying them securely so they could not escape again. Chapman bet that if he tied Angel up, there was no way he could escape.

CROSS-CURRENTS

Criss Angel's personal life is not without its problems. To find out more, read "Private Failures." Go to page 55. ▶▶

Angel took the challenge, and soon Dog and his assistants tied Angel to a chair using 100 feet of thick rope. When he was securely tied, Angel gave the okay and Dog pushed him into a swimming pool. Immediately, Angel busied himself, trying to get out of the ropes. But it was clear that Dog was a master of tying knots. These were much more difficult than any Angel had ever encountered. To make things worse, Angel later explained to *Luxe Life Celebrity News*, the ropes became tighter when they got wet:

After Criss debuted the third season of his show, A&E executives reported that its popularity had meant an increase in audience numbers for the cable network. *Criss Angel: Mindfreak* attracted 2.7 million viewers to its third season premiere. It was the number one show for adults in the 18- to 49-year-old age group for that time period.

Criss being sawed in half—in the open and without the cover of a magician's box. He performed this stunt during the first season of *Mindfreak* and in 2007 on an episode of *CSI: NY*. The *CSI* "Sleight Out of Hand" episode, which first aired February 28, 2007, featured Criss as Luke Blade, a famous magician whose assistants die suspiciously.

> **"I'd forgotten that water swells rope and thus tightens the knots even tighter than he had already tied them. I've practiced holding my breath underwater and can comfortably do four minutes, but that's without thrashing around trying to escape from something that tight."**

⟫ "I COMPLETELY FAILED" ⟪

The water in the pool became murky, and it was hard to see Angel's progress. But the clock told the story. As the time went to two minutes, then three, people became nervous. Some staffers suggested pulling Angel from the water.

Just after four minutes underwater, Angel emerged and spectators applauded. But clearly, he was not happy. He had removed some of the ropes on his feet and hands, but he was still tied to the chair. He had not been able to undo the ropes around his waist. Angel smacked the water angrily, frustrated with himself for not completing the escape.

He expressed that frustration to the *Mindfreak* cameras:

❝Despite the applause, I felt completely defeated. This was the first time that I completely failed.❞

⇒ MAKE-A-WISH ⇐

There is one group of fans that is not at all troubled if Criss Angel fails from time to time. They are children whom Angel has helped in

Criss Angel poses with young fans in 2007. Since the first season of *Mindfreak* aired in 2005, Criss has won lots of devoted fans who look forward to seeing the program continue for many more seasons. Members of the Criss Angel official fan club refer to themselves as loyal freaks, or simply the Loyal.

the Make-a-Wish Foundation. The foundation has been working hard since 1980 to make wishes come true for kids with life-threatening diseases. A lot of them say their biggest wish is to spend a little time with Angel.

Criss has donated countless hours meeting with children and teaching them magic tricks. Sometimes, if a child is too tired to participate in the excitement, he is happy just to sit quietly and talk. A number of children have been flown out to Las Vegas at his expense. Angel makes sure that the children and their families get to watch a taping of *Mindfreak*, too.

In 2007 Angel was honored by the foundation with its Chris Grecius Award, given each year to the celebrity who has donated the most money or time to the Make-a-Wish children. Blinking back tears, he told reporters that the award meant more to him than he could ever express:

> **It's the best and most meaningful award I have ever received. I can't exactly tell you how this feels. I am so honored, and it's the proudest I've ever been.**

⇒ WHERE IDEAS COME FROM ⇐

As Criss Angel gets more and more famous, he seems to be working harder than ever. He has never slept more than a few hours a night, and the rest of his time is devoted to building his act—just as when he was just starting out. Even though he now has a large staff of technical advisors and other assistants, he still designs his own tricks and illusions.

Angel says that he most enjoys developing an idea that seems impossible at first—even to him. Many of his ideas come when he is most relaxed, such as just before he falls asleep at night. One impossible-sounding idea for a trick came to him as he watched the ceiling fan in his room. As he watched the spinning fan, he thought about an illusion that involved reading someone's mind in a way never done before.

For example, in his autobiography Angel remembers thinking how amazing it would be if he could spontaneously make a fan stop and have the person's thoughts written in ashes on one of the fan's paddles:

"Impossible, right? Wrong. I actually figured out a way to make that one work.**"**

⇛ LOOKING AHEAD ⇚

Criss Angel looks to the future with excitement. In 2007 he signed a deal with the world-famous Cirque du Soleil. Never before has that organization put all of its energy and expertise behind one performer. He agreed to perform at the Luxor an eye-popping 4,600 shows over ten years, beginning in the summer of 2008—although he still intends to do new seasons of *Mindfreak*.

On March 22, 2007 it was announced that Criss would host a Cirque du Soleil show at the Luxor. The performance would combine his illusions and artistry with acrobatics, dance, puppetry, and music. Making the announcement, from left to right, were Felix Rappaport, Luxor Resort president; Criss Angel; Daniel Lamarre, president of Cirque du Soleil; and Gilles Ste-Croix, Cirque senior vice president.

The future looks bright for illusionist Criss Angel, who has received much recognition for his talents. In February 2008 he took home the Merlin Award for Magician of the Year from the International Magicians Society, which claims to be the world's largest magic society. He previously won the Merlin, which recognizes excellence in magic, in 2001, 2004, and 2007.

In 2008 Angel was also informed that he would be presented with the Magician of the Decade award by the International Magicians Society (IMS). He has won the IMS's golden Merlin statue (like an Oscar, but for magicians) four times. He is the only magician ever to win the award in back-to-back years.

But the future is expanding beyond magic, too. Angel is starring in a new movie called *Mandrake*, due out in late 2008. It is based on the adventures of an old comic-book character who fights crime by using his incredible skills as a magician. Angel will be playing Mandrake's father, Theron. He will also be designing and creating all the visual effects for the movie.

It is hard to imagine how one person could do as much as Criss Angel, and do it with as much enthusiasm and determination. One thing is certain: It is not sleight of hand. His success is no mere illusion.

The Origin of *Mindfreak*

One of the biggest challenges was the name of the show. Criss Angel did not want it to sound stereotyped—that seemed old-fashioned, something that would not draw young crowds. Besides, though he loved magic, he had never felt comfortable calling himself a magician. He needed a word that sounded edgier, more exciting. It needed to reflect his new kind of magic.

Criss considered words like *mystifier* and *illusionist*, but they did not seem quite right, either. He decided to make up his own word—*mindfreak*—as he explains in his autobiography:

"I knew my performances were considered to be a little freaky. I intentionally design my demonstrations to manipulate people's minds—play with their heads. Some people even believe I'm a spooky guy with supernatural powers, which makes me a freak of nature. I began playing with all of these words, twisting them around, tying them together, and breaking them apart until I had an epiphany."

The word *mindfreak* seemed so right to Angel that he has used it in almost every project—his off-Broadway show, his autobiography, the specials he has done for various networks, and his hit series on the A&E network. (Go back to page 6.) ◀◀

The Greatest Ever

The great magician Harry Houdini had a profound influence on Criss Angel's career. Houdini was born Ehrich Weisz (later changed to Weiss) on March 24, 1874, in Budapest, Hungary. In 1878 his family immigrated to the United States and settled in Appleton, Wisconsin. Ehrich, wanting to be considered an American, would forever tell people that he had been born in Appleton.

Ehrich became fascinated with magic at the age of eight, when his father took him to a traveling magic show. He performed for the first time later that year, doing a few physical stunts, such as tricks on a trapeze. For his show, he called himself "Ehrich, the Prince of the Air." When he was 15, he read an autobiography of a French magician, Jean Robert-Houdin. From then on, out of admiration for Robert-Houdin, he began using the name Houdini when he performed.

Houdini spent the first years as a performer developing his talents. He was a superb swimmer and could also do many gymnastic tricks. He was good at card tricks and illusions. But what interested him the most was escape. He had always been good at picking locks. As a young boy, he had opened a locked cupboard and stolen a fresh apple pie his mother had made. This talent, he believed, could work well in a magic show.

Soon Houdini was making a name for himself as the greatest escape artist ever. Every town he visited, he would offer to pay $100 to anyone who could produce a pair of handcuffs from which he could not escape. No one could.

Harry Houdini gained fame for escaping from handcuffs and straitjacket restraints, breaking out of jails, and for performing death-defying feats. In the early 1900s, he performed throughout Europe, promoting himself as the World's Handcuff King and Prison Breaker. One of the escape artist's posters proclaimed: "Nothing on earth can hold Houdini a prisoner."

Even when his show traveled to England in 1900 and he was placed in the cuffs used by Scotland Yard, he had no trouble escaping.

As Houdini's reputation grew, it was clear audiences could not get enough of him. By 1900 he was making more than $2,000 per week. But it was important to add to his act, so audiences would keep coming back. He began doing dangerous stunts. In one escape, he jumped into San Francisco Bay, his wrists in police handcuffs and his ankle shackled to a 75-pound ball. He invented the Chinese Water Torture Cell, a container filled with water, and successfully escaped.

Houdini had always claimed he could withstand the punch of any man because his stomach muscles were so strong. But one man surprised him by punching him before Houdini had a chance to tighten those muscles. That ruptured his appendix, and he developed a serious infection. He died on Halloween at the age of 52. (Go back to page 12.) ◀◀

Fantasizing

In his autobiography, *Mindfreak*, Criss Angel wrote about about his desire to be famous when he was a young boy. As he explains, he was not really sure about how he would achieve his fame. It could have been magic, music, or even being a stuntman—whatever put him in front of the public eye:

A portion of the promotional poster for season three of Criss Angel: Mindfreak, *which premiered in June 2007. Two months earlier saw the publication of the illusionist's first book,* Mindfreak: Secret Revelations, *from Harper Collins. It provides background information on Criss as well as instructions on how to perform some of his tricks.*

"My intense drive, insatiable hunger, and quest for success have been part of my personality from the day I was born. I so desperately wanted to achieve my dreams, I didn't care how it came. I'd do whatever I could to be in front of an audience. . . . I wanted to do it all—model, act, juggle, ride a unicycle, eat cereal in front of the camera—whatever it took to do this for a living. . . . I fantasized about fame all the time. I usually found myself staring out the window of our family van, imagining myself on all of the billboards that dotted the sides of the Long Island Expressway. I daydreamed it was me up there in the Calvin Klein or Coca-Cola ads. I'd imagine my face on the body of the models. I'd try to feel what it was like to have thousands of people stare at a billboard with my image on it." (Go back to page 12.) ◀◀

Rejection

Criss believes his popularity reflects his success in using artistry in magic. He has said, "I always felt that magic was a beautiful art form, but magicians killed it because of their hokey presentations. But I believed that if you presented the art of magic outside the box it would be limitless and finally garner the respect that it deserves."

As Criss Angel explains in his autobiography, *Mindfreak*, during the early days neither his music nor his magic was an instant hit. He had plenty of rejection, and he found it very painful:

"So many critics just didn't get me. I was different from anyone they'd ever seen. . . . I was told numerous times they didn't like the gothic image and they didn't think I was talented enough. Some even said I was too gross to be entertaining. I used to get so upset by the rejection. I'd literally lie in my bed and cry for hours because some record executive promised he'd call me and never did. . . . It took me years to understand and accept that when something doesn't happen as you'd like it to, it usually means that there is a better scenario in the future.

I kept all of the rejection letters I received over the years as my personal inspiration to prove to those doubters they were wrong. For years, their dismissive words brewed in my mind. Ultimately, I realized the negative responses actually had a positive influence. Rejection helps you narrow down and focus on the areas of your life that move you, that propel you toward the right path."

(Go back to page 18.) ◀◀

A Learning Process

Criss has been called the master of street magic. Some of his stunts, like this one featuring a woman who has been "pulled apart," take place on the sidewalks and in the parks of Las Vegas. Criss's technique of working up close and personal with his audience has helped make Mindfreak *the most successful magic show in television history.*

During an interview early in his career with Kira Billik of the *Cleveland Plain Dealer*, Angel discussed some of the ideas he had for illusions in future acts. Vanishing large objects was exciting for audiences, he told her, and so he planned to do the ultimate vanish—making the audience disappear. He also planned to escape from a straitjacket while hanging upside down from a helicopter next to the Statue of Liberty:

"I'm planning on floating out over the audience and being able to float down and touch people's hands. I'm planning on cutting a girl [in half] with a chainsaw without any boxes, without any tables. She will be standing . . . and I will cut her as you cut a tree down. Her feet will run away from her and her upper body will go to the floor.

I hope I can put her back together—I haven't worked out that part yet. I'll be going through a lot of girls, I'm sure, in the beginning."

(Go back to page 25.)

Empowering the Audience

In his interview with Steve West for the Web site Blend Television, Angel explained that when he does a dangerous stunt, he hopes it can benefit the viewers:

"One of the most gratifying things I get as an artist is when people watch me do these different demonstrations, and they in some way feel empowered by what I'm doing so they can confront their own fears. Maybe it's the fear of getting in an elevator; maybe it's the fear of going on a plane and seeing the world. But the greatest gift I get is when somebody comes up to me or mails me and says, 'Criss, I watched this and I got help.' Or, 'I'm able to do something I couldn't do, and I can live my life a little richer or a little fuller than I did prior to seeing that demonstration.' That's what the great Houdini did. Houdini connected to people on an emotional level so that when he would escape that straitjacket it wasn't about the straitjacket. It was about people looking at it and escaping poverty. When you have that, it's the truest form of magic."

(Go back to page 31.)

Criss Angel performs a levitation stunt during the filming of one of the episodes for Mindfreak. *The illusionist appears to fly up and float in the air without the help of any wires or other supporting devices or the use of special equipment. On his show he has also levitated volunteers.*

Trainfreak? Carfreak?

Since his *Mindfreak* series, Criss Angel has become wealthy. It has not changed the way he dresses—he rarely is seen in anything but T-shirts and jeans. He does not buy much jewelry, and works too much to travel. He does admit, however, to spending money on a couple of things about which he is passionate—vehicles. As he told *Chicago Tribune* reporter Nina Metz during an interview:

> **"I have the most insane Lionel train set, with houses and a whole city, an amusement park, with a moving Ferris wheel, a helicopter port, a house in the country that goes on fire. I've been collecting this now for a while, and yes, I absolutely play with it."**

Criss is also wild about bigger "toys." He owns more than 20 motorcycles. He has several go-carts that can move at more than 150 miles per hour. But his cars are his pride and joy.

> **"I just got a brand new—one of fourteen in the world—custom-made black Rolls-Royce Phantom with an extended back. I get driven in that one. I also have a Lamborghini 2007 Murcielago LP640, and that's like my personal car. [It retails for $320,000.] I have a [Dodge] Viper that is all tricked out. And I have a Mindfreak Hummer, which is currently on tour, going to car shows."**

(Go back to page 35.)

Debunking the Fakes

Though he is usually very mild-mannered and easygoing, Criss is angered by people who claim to have supernatural powers. Some say they can communicate with the dead, others say that they can heal someone with just a touch. It makes him especially angry because it is usually very desperate people who seek out those who make such claims—people who are terminally ill or their families, for example. They are all charlatans, or fakes, he says in his autobiography:

> **"A lot of people have made big money by presenting themselves as having some kinds of paranormal gift. This phenomenon exists because of the most basic human need to want to believe. At its core, faith is the belief in something you cannot see but know, without a doubt, exists. I can get behind faith from a religious standpoint, but I cannot support the charlatans who go around masquerading as psychic, clairvoyant, . . . telepathic, channelers, mediums, communicators to the 'other side,' and every other type of supposed paranormal or supernatural being who preys on human weakness and vulnerability for personal gain. If these people truly existed, why didn't they predict the catastrophes of Hurricane Katrina, 9/11, or the Holocaust?"**

(Go back to page 38.) ◀◀

Private Failures

In 2007 newspapers began reporting a story that bewildered Criss Angel's fans. According to the media, Angel's wife was suing him for divorce. What made the story so confusing was that no one seemed to have ever heard that Angel was married. So how could he be getting a divorce?

As it turned out, Criss did indeed have a wife. She was Joanne Winkhart, who had dated Angel for almost 10 years before they married in 2002. She claimed that he had distanced himself from her when he became famous. He had not supported her at all, she said, even though he had been earning millions of dollars in recent years.

Winkhart's father, actor Richard Winkhart, told reporters that he was angry at the way Angel had treated her:

> **"When his career took a jump forward, he became a different person. My daughter was never acknowledged as his wife. He told her it was . . . better [for him to have] a single image, than a married image."**

Joanne Winkhart was especially hurt, her father told reporters, that Angel had been seen in the company of a number of other women. Angel did not comment—either on the charges against him, nor on his marriage to Winkhart.

(Go back to page 40.)

Criss was married in 2002 and separated from his wife in 2006. Since then, he has been linked with celebrities like Paris Hilton, Lindsay Lohan, and Cameron Diaz. In August 2006, Criss responded to gossip about a relationship with Britney Spears (shown here in a photo with Criss) by explaining he was helping her prepare for an MTV Video Music Awards performance.

1967   Christopher Nicholas Sarantakos is born on Long Island, New York, December 19.

1974   His Aunt Stella shows him his first card trick and explains how it works.

1979   Criss lands his first paying job as a magician at a neighborhood birthday party.

1981   He begins working at the Wine Gallery as a table magician.

1994   Angel makes an appearance on an ABC special called *Secrets*.

1995   Angel's father is diagnosed with stomach cancer and is given three weeks to live.

1998   Angel performs in *Criss Angel: World of Illusion* at Madison Square Garden and makes $50,000 selling signed memorabilia.

His father dies three years after being diagnosed with cancer.

2001   Angel scores and performs in the off-Broadway show *Criss Angel Mindfreak*.

2002   Angel marries longtime girlfriend Joanne Winkhart.

To promote the television special *Mindfreak*, he is suspended by hooks and hangs in the Superman position for six hours in Times Square.

2003   The Sci-Fi Channel airs *Supernatural*.

2004   David Baram becomes Angel's manager.

2005   *Mindfreak* premieres on the A&E Television network.

2007   Angel's wife, Joanne Winkhart, files for divorce.

Mindfreak: Secret Revelations, Criss Angel's autobiography and a behind-the-scenes look at his magic, is released and makes the *New York Times* bestseller list.

2008   Angel's technical staff begins working with Cirque du Soleil in preparation for the new Cirque act opening in Las Vegas in summer 2008.

Television Appearances

1994 ABC's *Secrets*

2002 *Good Morning America*, Water Torture Cell performance
"Criss Angel Mindfreak," part of ABC's *Thirteen Nights of Halloween*

2003 Sci-Fi Channel's *Supernatural*
Criss Angel: Made in Japan, two-hour Japanese television special

2005 *Criss Angel Mindfreak,* A&E

2006 *Criss Angel Mindfreak,* A&E

2007 *Criss Angel Mindfreak,* A&E
NBC's reality show *Phenomenon*
CSI: New York, played a killer in one episode
Larry King Live, two episodes

Live Performances

1998 *Criss Angel: World of Illusion*, Madison Square Garden Halloween event

2001 *Criss Angel Mindfreak*, off-Broadway show

2002 *Criss Angel Mindfreak*, off-Broadway show
Times Square body-suspension performance

2003 *Criss Angel Mindfreak*, off-Broadway show

2008 Criss Angel/Cirque du Soleil show in Las Vegas

Awards

2001 Magician of the Year, International Magicians Society

2003 Silver Telly Award for *Criss Angel: Made in Japan*

2004 Magician of the Year, International Magicians Society

2007 Magician of the Year, International Magicians Society
Chris Grecius Award, Make-a-Wish Foundation

2008 Magician of the Year, International Magicians Society
Magician of the Decade, International Magicians Society

Movie

2008 *Mandrake*

Book

2007 *Mindfreak: Secret Revelations*

Books

Angel, Criss, with Laura Morton. *Mindfreak: Secret Revelations*. New York: HarperCollins, 2007.

Fleischman, Sid. *Escape! The Story of the Great Houdini*. New York: Greenwillow, 2006.

Stefoff, Rebecca. *Magic*. New York: Marshall Cavendish Benchmark, 2008.

Periodicals

Metz, Nina. "It's No Illusion—That's a Train Set in His Pad." *Chicago Tribune* (May 20, 2007): p. 9.

Oldenburg, Ann. "Poof! Criss Angel Has Turned into the Magician of the Moment." *USA Today* (August 3, 2005): p. D3.

Williams, Stephen. "Hot? This Guy Is on Fire." *Newsday* (October 24, 2005): p. B5.

Web Sites

http://www.aetv.com/criss_angel

This *Criss Angel Mindfreak* site from the A&E Television network has photos, news about Angel, information about each episode of *Mindfreak*, and videoclips of the most popular illusions.

http://www.crissangel.com

The official Web site of Criss Angel includes news about Angel's career, new illusions, *Mindfreak* merchandise, and information on "the Loyal," his most devoted fans.

http://www.houdinitribute.com

This amazing site, the Harry Houdini Tribute, not only includes a good biography of Houdini but also individual tricks that he performed and lots of photographs—even recordings of Houdini's voice during one of his acts.

http://www.magic-tricks-tips.com/criss-agel.html

This Web site, Magic Trick Tips, has links to stories of famous magicians and their signature tricks as well as a biography and information about Criss Angel.

http://www.mightytricks.com/2006/05/14.html

The Mighty Magic Tricks Web site offers dozens of tricks anyone can learn—tricks using money, handkerchiefs, and cards.

---

adrenaline—a chemical in the body that is produced when a person confronts danger.

allocate—to set aside.

candlepower—the intensity of a light source, as described in units called candelas.

choreography—the planning of dance or movement.

embedded—placed deeply in something.

filtration—the process of cleaning water by removing particles from it.

hologram—a three-dimensional image.

illusion—something that tricks the mind by appearing to be real when it actually is not.

levitating—floating in air.

off-Broadway—theatrical production, often experimental and performed in a small theater outside the Broadway entertainment district.

pyrotechnics—the craft of creating fireworks displays.

shackled—chained or restrained.

suspension—hanging.

tarantula—a large, hairy spider.

venture—an undertaking that involves some risk.

page 6 "Magic is a wonderful . . ." Susan Karlin, "The Daredevil." *Forbes* (July 4, 2005), p. 130.

page 9 "If you're watching . . ." Carolyn Spencer, telephone interview with author (March 16, 2008).

page 12 "It just boggled my mind . . ." Criss Angel with Laura Morton, *Mindfreak: Secret Revelations* (New York: HarperCollins, 2007), p. 29.

page 15 "Kids get fed . . ." Kira Billik, "Rocker Has Tricks of His Own." *Cleveland Plain Dealer* (May 20, 1994), p. 39.

page 15 "Everything I do . . ." Angel and Morton, *Mindfreak*, p. 70.

page 20 "He believed that his body . . . " Reg Seeton, "Criss Angel," Underground Online. http://www.ugo.com/ channels.dvd/features/crissangel/ interview.asp.

page 22 "Some people claimed . . ." Angel and Morton, *Mindfreak*, p. 26.

page 25 "When Christopher made his escape . . ." Angel and Morton, *Mindfreak*, p. 60.

page 25 "He was white . . ." Ralph R. Ortega, "Daredevil's Collapse Caps Water Tank Stunt." *New York Daily News* (August 28, 2002), p. 7.

page 28 "I enlisted the help . . ." Angel and Morton, *Mindfreak*, p. 134.

page 28 "From the moment I met . . ." Angel and Morton, *Mindfreak*, p. 137.

page 31 "In season one . . ." Seeton, "Criss Angel."

page 32 "I couldn't figure out . . ." *Criss Angel Mindfreak: The Complete Season Two*. DVD. Directed by Criss Angel. Produced by Angel Productions Inc. (New York: A&E Home Video, 2006).

page 35 "He has to escape . . ." *Criss Angel Mindfreak: The Complete Season Two*. DVD.

page 37 "The first season [of *Mindfreak*] . . ." Steve West, "Interview with the Mindfreak." Blend Television (June 3, 2007). http://www.cinemablend.com/ television/Interview-With-The-Mindfreak-Criss-Angel-4529.html.

page 38 "The debate of real versus . . . " Angel and Morton, *Mindfreak*, p. 13.

page 38 "I thought that it would . . ." West, "Interview with the Mindfreak."

page 40 "If I don't get fried . . ." *Criss Angel Mindfreak: The Complete Season Three*. DVD. Directed by Criss Angel. Produced by Angel Productions Inc. (New York: A&E Home Video, 2007).

page 42 "I'd forgotten that water swells . . ." Robin Leach, "'Mindfreak' Criss Angel Nearly Drowns While Filming in Las Vegas." http://www.vegaspopular.com/ 2007/02/27/mindfreak-criss-angel-nearly-drowns-while-filming-in-las-vegas.

page 43 "Despite the applause . . ." *Criss Angel Mindfreak: The Complete Season Three*. DVD.

page 44 "It's the best . . ." Robin Leach, "Criss Angel Celebrates His Birthday and Grants Last Wishes to the Make a Wish Children!" http://blogs.lasvegasmagazine.com/ VegasLuxeLife/criss-angel-celebrates-his-birthday-and-grants-last-wishes-to-the-make-a-wish-children.

page 45 "Impossible, right? . . ." Angel and Morton, *Mindfreak*, p. 110.

page 48 "I knew my performances . . ." Angel and Morton, *Mindfreak*, p. 109.

page 50 "My intense drive . . ." Angel and Morton, *Mindfreak*, p. 31, 33.

page 51 "So many critics . . ." Angel and Morton, *Mindfreak*, p. 97–98.

page 52 "I'm planning on floating . . ." Billik, "Rocker Has Tricks of His Own," p. 39.

page 53 "One of the most gratifying . . ." West, "Interview with the Mindfreak.

page 54 "I have the most insane . . ." Nina Metz, "It's No Illusion—That's a Train Set in His Pad." *Chicago Tribune* (May 20, 2007): p. 9.

page 54 "I just got a brand-new . . ." Metz, "It's No Illusion—That's a Train Set in His Pad," p. 9.

page 54 "A lot of people . . ." Angel and Morton, *Mindfreak*, p. 144.

page 55 "When his career . . . " "The One Thing Cameron's New Beau Can't Magic Away—His Wife." *Daily Mail* (July 1, 2007). http://www.dailymail.co.uk/pages/live/articles/showbiznews.html?in_article_id=465380&in_page_id=1773.

Gail Stewart has written more than 250 books for children and teens. She lives in Minneapolis, Minnesota. She is the mother of three sons—only one of whom can do any magic tricks.

PICTURE CREDITS

page

1: Luxor/Cirque Du Soleil/NMI

4: S. Lovekin/WireImage

7: A&E/PRMS

8: A&E/PRMS

10: ASP Library

13: Hal Schele/AMA/CIC Photos

14: StarMax Photos

16: Getty Images

19: Miller Brewing Co./NMI

21: A&E/FPS

23: Getty Images

24: Genii/NMI

26: Sci Fi Channel/FPS

29: A&E/PRMS

30: A&E/PRMS

33: A&E/PRMS

34: Splash News

36: A&E/PRMS

39: Luxor/FPS

41: A&E/PRMS

42: A&E/PRMS

43: Woodrow/CIC Photos

45: Luxor/Cirque Du Soleil/NMI

46: Jemal Countess/WireImage

49: New Millennium Images

50: A&E/PRMS

51: A&E/FPS

52: A&E/PRMS

53: A&E/PRMS

55: Osdia/CIC Photos

Front cover: A&E/PRMS